HUNGARIAN

kitchen the simple way

Soups

Main Courses

Desserts

Traditional Goulash Soup

Traditionally this soup is cooked over the open fire in a cauldron. This soup is normally served as a starter or small lunch. I, personally, eat it as a main dish together with fresh white bread and enjoy the spicy aroma.

serves 4
takes 150 minutes

SOUP
3 onions, finely chopped
3 tbsp Lard
400 grams beef , cubed
2 1/2 l water
3 tsp salt
2 tbsp Hungarian paprika
1 tomato, peeled, chopped
1 yellow pepper, chopped
1 parsnip, diced
1 carrot, diced
1 green pepper, chopped
2 garlic cloves, mashed
4 potatoes, cubed
2 tsp cumin
1/2 tsp black pepper
some parsley, finely chopped.
PINCHED NOODLES
1 egg, 12 tbsp flour
pinch of salt,
 2 tbsp oil

Sauté the onion in lard until golden. Add Hungarian paprika and 10 ml water.

Once the water boils add the beef and stir until well browned. Add some water, cumin and black pepper.

Boil it for 50 minutes and add water many times while the meat softens.

Then add parsnip, carrot, yellow paprika and tomatoes. Cook for another 40 minutes and add potatoes, salt, green pepper, garlic and pour more water (for soup consistency). Bring to the boil for another 15 minutes.

MAKE PINCHED NOODLES: Combine ingredients with enough flour to make a firm dough. Let dough sit for 5 minutes. Roll dough and pinch off dime sized pieces. Add Pinched Noodles and boil a few minutes longer. When the noodles float to the surface, they are done.

Serve it with chopped parsley sprinkled on each portion.

Jókai Bean Soup

Another one of my favourites - who says frugal can't taste fantastic? Jókai Mór (1825–1904), was a Hungarian dramatist and novelist. This soup was named after him. Soak the beans overnight (longer but uses no energy) or do the rapid soak - cover with water and bring to a boil, simmer 20 minutes, turn off heat, cover & let sit for an hour.

serves 6
takes 150 minutes

1-2 pig's trotters (800g), smoked
150 g pork ribs, smoked
1 celery, peeled, diced
250 g beans
1 medium parsnip, diced
1 medium carrot, diced
1 onion, peeled, chopped
1 tbsp lard
1 tbsp parsley, chopped
3 tbsp flour
1 1/2 tbsp Hungarian paprika
2 garlic cloves, mashed
2 bay leaves
250 g smoked kolbász
(Hungarian dried sausage)
salt and pepper to taste
6 tbsp sour cream

Cook smoked pig's trotters and pork ribs in 2 litres water till the meat comes of the bones. Debone them and put meat pieces aside.

Add the diced celery, parsnip, carrot and the beans to the meat broth, cook till beans are done.

In the meantime, fry onion in lard over low heat. Once the onion is wilted, add chopped parsley and flour and make a brown roux over the lowest heat possible. Stir often to prevent burning. When the roux is light brown, mix in paprika and garlic; immediately add 1 cup cold water. Whip till smooth, then pour into the cooked beans.

Add smoked sausage. Simmer for 10 minutes. Cut smoked meats into small pieces, and add to the soup.

Adjust salt and pepper.

Add the sour cream. Serve with little Pinched Dumplings (see Goulash recipe).

Chicken Soup Újházy style

Once upon a time, a great Hungarian actor in the 19th century had a yen for making soup–his own Hungarian version of the French poule au pot. To ensure a concentrated flavour, Újházy Ede (1844-1915) used a whole chicken, then added vegetables that differed markedly in colour, shape, and texture. It contained a whole chicken, because he believed none of it should be wasted.

serves 5-6
takes 120 minutes

1 chicken (1,5 kg) cut
3 small carrots, peeled
2 young parsnips, peeled
1 whole celery root, peeled
and cut into cubes
100 g mushroom
2 onions peeled
2 garlic cloves, chopped
slice of ginger root
1 tomato peeled, chopped
1 green Hungarian pepper
(long, thin, and spicy)
1/2 head cauliflower, broken
into flowerets
100 g green peas, chopped
soup noodles (which are
served separately)
1 tsp peppercorns
salt to taste

Clean the chicken and cut it into eight pieces. Include the neck, and gizzard as well.

Add cold water and cook to a boil, then remove foam.

Add salt, onions, garlic, tomato and spices and continue to cook on low heat for about an hour.

When the meat starts to soften, add vegetables, thinly sliced mushroom, cauliflower, the carrots, celery root, ginger, parsnips and green pepper. If you use fresh green peas, add with the rest of the vegetables, if they are canned, then only add at the end with the liver.

Simmer it for another 10 - 15 minutes. Before serving, add soup pasta cooked separately in salted water. Serve with the meat and vegetables and offer vinegary horseradish on the side.

Cherry Soup

Ripe cherries are a special seasonal treat in Hungary. Sour Cherries have a wonderful flavour when cooked. Some families like to make their soup with sweet cream instead of sour cream. Some add a little sherry. However you make this soup, you will enjoy its refreshing flavour.

serves 3-4
takes 30 minutes

1 kg of fresh pitted sour cherries (Do not use canned)
1 1/2 litres water
2 tbsp flour
1 cup sour cream or sweet cream
pinch of salt
5 cm stick of cinnamon
couple of cloves
150 g of sugar

Into a soup pot containing 1 1/2 litres of boiling water add salt, cinnamon bark, cloves, sugar. In 3 minutes add fresh sour cherries. Stir and cook for one minute.

In a separate bowl mix flour, sour cream and beat until smooth. Add to flour mix, 1 cup of hot cherry sugar mix. Stir well.

Add the flour, sour cream and hot cherry mix into the pot of hot soup, stir well and simmer for 5 or 6 minutes until thickened.

Cover the soup and let cool. Keep cover on while chilling in refrigerator to prevent formation of a thick skin. Serve very cold.

Note: To make Cherry Soup with Sweet Cream cook a 5 cm stick of cinnamon with the cherries, and substitute sweet cream for the sour cream. Discard cinnamon stick when done cooking soup. Chill as above.

Hungarian Fisherman's Soup

The simplest way of preparing a meal is often the best – this motto certainly applies to this delicious fish soup. Cook, if possible, on open wood-fire to add smoke flavour to it.

serves 4
takes 40 minutes

1 kg freshwater fish
1 big onion, chopped
1 litre water
1 1/2   tbsp Hungarian Paprika
1 small Hungarian hot pepper
or chilli
salt to taste

Scale, chop up, clean and salt the fish. Do not wash the blood off!

Place the fish chops in a cauldron with their meat upside down. Leave them there for one hour.

Add the onion and pour in 1 litre cold water and boil over a strong heat.

When the water boils add 1 tbsp of Hungarian paprika and one hot Hungarian red pepper chilli pepper and cook for 25 minutes without stirring or covering with a lid.

Five minutes before it is finished add another teaspoon of paprika and salt to taste.

Stuffed Chicken

This is not for any one who is counting calories. This stuffing brings out the flavour of chicken, turkey or veal. I am sure that once you taste this it will become your favourite also.

serves 5
takes 50 minutes

1 chicken about 1,5 kg
70 grams mushrooms
30 grams lard or chicken fat
40 g smoked bacon, diced
2 small eggs
3 dry bread rolls
1/2 L milk
1/2 tsp ground white pepper
1 tbsp Hungarian paprika
1 small onion, chopped
a bunch of parsley, chopped
salt to taste
1/2 tsp marjoram

Carefully separate the skin from chicken, starting at the neck. Salt the inside of the chicken and the meat under the skin.

Chop mushrooms and onion and fry them in bacon fat.

Soak the rolls in milk, crumble them and mix with an egg, salt, pepper, browned onion, marjoram, Hungarian paprika, parsley, fried bacon cubes and mushrooms.

Use force to spread part of this stuffing under the chicken skin and put the rest inside the chicken.

Heat the chicken fat in a roasting tin and brown the chicken on each side. Cover the tin with foil or a lid, place in an oven at 180 °C for about 1 hour, basting occasionally.

Let the chicken rest for 25-30 minutes before carving, to give the stuffing time to set.

Serve it with Hungarian fried potatoes or rice.

Transylvanian mixed grill

Place the potato wedges in the middle of a large wooden platter (actually that's what "Erdélyi fatányéros" means: wooden platter from Transylvania!) then arrange the meat slices around them. If desired decorate the edges with lettuce leaves, freshly cut onion rings as well as tomato slices and yellow paprika cut into rings. Score the bacon and fry, which will turn it into the shape of a cock's comb, then sprinkle with paprika and place on top of the meats.

serves 4
takes 35 minutes

4 small slices pork chops
4 small slices veal chops
4 small slices sirloin steak
100 grams smoked bacon
(with skin on)
2 tbsp oil
4 potatoes for potato wedges
oil for frying potatoes
pinch of Hungarian paprika
salt & pepper
2 small tomatoes,
1 yellow pepper
lettuce leaves and an onion
sliced for decoration

Carefully clean, then tenderise the meat slices, season with salt and pepper.

Cut the bacon into four equal pieces, score the skin and then fry. The bacon pieces will turn into the cock's comb shape. Set bacon aside and keep warm. Fry the meat slices in hot oil on both sides till done.

At the same time prepare the potato wedges, making sure wedges and meats are ready for serving at the same time. Serve one piece of each kind of meat per person.

Decorate with the listed vegetables and serve. Do not forget to sprinkle meat tops and the cockscombs with paprika.

Hungarian Roast Goose Liver

serves 4
takes 30 minutes

1 kg fattened
goose liver
black peppercorns
150 g goose fat or lard
1-2 medium onions
500 ml milk
1 cup white wine
salt

Wash liver well, then soak in milk for an hour.

Remove and, dry with clean cloth, then sprinkle with salt.

Heat goose fat or lard in a pan, and fry goose liver in it for 5-8 minutes, until slightly brown, then add enough wine to cover half of it, the sliced onions, the pepper, and salt again.

Stew in the oven, covered with lid, until gravy is reduced.

Remove lid, and leave in the oven until liver is brown on all sides.

Set a bed of mashed potatoes in the middle of the dish, and lay the thinly sliced goose liver overtop when dishing.

Strain gravy through sieve, and pour some over the liver.

Dill-flavoured Cottage Cheese Dumplings

serves 4
takes 75 minutes

*800 g strained cottage
cheese
120 g semolina
salt to taste
pepper to taste
4 eggs
30 g (2 tbs) butter
¼ cup fresh chopped dill*

Mix strained cottage cheese with the eggs, semolina, a pinch of salt and pepper and half of the chopped dill.

Allow mixture to stand for about an hour. If the cottage cheese is dry, use less semolina.

Shape dumplings with moist hands and cook them in boiling salt water until they rise to the surface.

Melt the butter and add the other half of the chopped dill.

Place the dumplings on a preheated platter with the dill sauce poured over them.

Dill dumplings are often served with chicken paprikash.

Braised Beef Roll Csáky Style

This dish combines the flavours of Hungarian scrambled eggs with bacon, onion and peppers and a wine-braised roast with the ubiquitous sour cream.

serves 6
takes 60 minutes

1 kg beef steak
(eg. Sirloin, Rump)
1/2 cup mustard
1/2 cup oil or lard
300 g bacon
4 medium onions
1 tbsp Hungarian paprika
4 yellow peppers
2 plum tomatoes
3 medium eggs
1 cup sour cream
1 cup dry red wine
1/2 for the meat
the other half a drink
for the cook
salt and pepper to taste

Pickle the meat in mustard and oil for 2 days.

Dice bacon, chop onions, peel, seed and dice tomatoes. Slice peppers, beat eggs. Sauté bacon in some lard. Add the onions, sauté until transparent. Take off the heat, stir in sweet Hungarian paprika, then add yellow pepper and tomatoes. Season with salt and pepper.

Sauté until the liquid is gone. Add eggs and cook, stirring until firm.

Cut beef in wide slices, 1,5 cm thick or less. Tenderise carefully until 0,5 cm thick, without making holes.

Spread with the egg and pepper mixture, roll up, tuck in ends and tie up. Brown the meat rolls in hot oil or lard, continuously adding wine. Remove.

Serve the meat in diagonal slices with the sauce and small caps of sour cream. Serve with fried potatoes or rice and cucumber salad servieren.

Paprika Potatoes

Despite its title - Paprikás Krumpli -, this dish does contain meat, and it's meant to be served as a main course.

serves 4
takes 45 minutes

1 kg potatoes
2 large onions
50 grams smoked bacon
50 grams lard
100 grams smoked kolbász
(dry sausage)
2 tbsp Hungarian paprika
1 medium yellow paprika
sliced
1 tomato, diced
sour cream
salt to taste
pepper to taste

Melt the smoked bacon with one spoonful of the lard. Peel and then cut the onions into small cubes, sauté in the fat until they are clear.

Take the pan off of the heat and mix in the Hungarian paprika, some water and stir.

Peel the potatoes, wash them, and cut them into quarters.

Put potatoes, yellow paprika and tomato in the onions and fat, and return the pan to the stove and mix.

Pour water over top, salt, and add peppers. When almost ready, add the sausage, and cook it for a few more minutes.

Serve with sour cream.

Chicken Paprikash

Chicken appears in Hungarian cuisine often but it is never boring because there are so many ways to serve it. Authentic Chicken Paprikash never has tomatoes in it. Chicken Paprika Stew does. Make plenty of dumplings to go with it.

serves 4
takes 80 minutes

1 chicken, cut up
salt and pepper, to taste
2 tbsp Hungarian paprika
1 tbsp lard
1 large onion, chopped
1 tbsp flour
1 cup water
1 yellow paprika, chopped
1-2 tbsp sour cream

Season the chicken with salt.

Cut the onions into small pieces and lightly cook them in the lard. Then sprinkle them with Hungarian paprika.

Add the chicken (which has been cut into pieces), some water, and stir well.

Add fresh yellow paprika and peppers. Salt and sauté in a covered pot. Add water as required while the meat softens.

Before serving mix flour with the sour cream, adding it to the chicken, and bring it to a boil once more.

Serve with dumplings or mashed potatoes.

Tomato Stuffed with Chicken

serves 3
takes 47 minutes

6 medium-size fresh crispy
tomatoes
3/4 tsp salt
1 tbsp finely chopped onion
3 tbsp butter
20 g cooked, chopped
chicken breast
4 tbsp wheat, rice, or corn
cereal
1 tsp paprika powder
3 cloves garlic, mashed
6 sprigs parsley

Wash tomatoes; remove thin slice from stem end of each.

Scoop out pulp; save.

Sprinkle inside of tomatoes with 1/4 teaspoon salt; invert tomatoes to drain excess liquid for 30 minutes.

Fry onion in 2 tablespoons butter in large pan until lightly browned, for about 5 minutes.

Add 1 1/4 cup tomato pulp, chicken, garlic, salt, and paprika powder; cook for 3 minutes, stirring often.

Fill each tomato with stuffing. Mix crushed cereal flakes with melted butter; sprinkle over tomatoes.

Place tomatoes on baking sheet.

Bake for 30 minutes in preheated 200°C oven.

Garnish with parsley.

Pasta With Cottage Cheese

This recipe is great for nights when you get home and need something to eat while winding down. 'Turos Csusza' is a Hungarian dish, which normally accompanies fish meals. Made well, this dish will surely bring a wide smile to the consumers face.

serves 4
takes 22 minutes

500 grams package egg noodles
100 grams slices smoked bacon
2 cups sour cream
500 grams container cottage cheese
1/4 tsp salt, to taste
1 tsp oil
pinch of pepper

Bring a large pot of lightly salted water to a boil, then add pasta, some oil & cook until al dente, about 8-10 minutes.

Drain well.

Cut the bacon into small cubes.

In a skillet, over medium-high heat, cook bacon until crisp, about 8-10 minutes, then drain, set aside.

In a 2-quart casserole, place drained noodles, then stir sour cream into the noodles.

Spoon cottage cheese evenly over the top of the noodle mixture and sprinkle bacon pieces over top.

Season to taste with salt and pepper.

Hungarian Macaroni

serves 4
takes 60 minutes

80 g (3 slices)
smoked bacon
50 g lard
150 g onion
1 tbsp paprika
500 g veal
salt to taste
4 cloves garlic, chopped
140 g diced green pepper
60 g tomato
600 g macaroni
120 g grated cheese

Fry until the bacon fat is translucent.

Add the chopped onion and fry until light brown.

Add the paprika, then immediately add the meat, which is cut approximately into pea size.

Add salt and garlic; if too dry, add a small amount of water.

When the meat is almost done, add the green peppers and tomato cut into small cubes.

Simmer until almost all of the liquid is used up. Cook the macaroni and add to the meat.

Place the mixture in an ovenproof dish and sprinkle with cheese.

Bake in the oven for a few minutes, until cheese melts on top.

Potato Dumplings With Cabbage

Káposztás sztrapacska is a Palóc speciality. The Palóc are an ethnic minority group in north-east Hungary. These potato dumplings are also often made with curd cheese. Usually eaten on their own, they can also be served as a side dish to meats.

serves 4
takes 55 minutes

1 kg potatoes
1/2 kg flour
2 tbsp oil
1/2 kg cabbage
2 tbsp granulated sugar
salt and pepper to taste

Grate and salt the cabbage. Put aside for 28 min. The salt will soften the cabbage.

Squeeze juice out of the cabbage. In a pan brown it in oil with sugar.

Take peeled and grated potatoes and mix with flour to make a light dough.

Using a spatula press batter through a spaetzle maker or sieve with bigger holes into boiling water. The noodles are done when they float to the top.

Drain, then transfer to an oiled dish and mix with cabbage.

Serve with pepper sprinkled on top and season with salt.

Diced Pork Brassó Style

Brassói aprópecsenye, as this dish is called in Hungarian, is very easy to prepare. Save time by using boneless pork chops and cube them after they are browned. Use high quality, real Hungarian paprika for best results. Enjoy a simple but very tasty meal, scented with the fragrance of rich Hungarian paprika and fresh yellow peppers.

serves 3-4
takes 45 minutes

500 g meat, cut into
1,5-2 cm cubes
5 tbsp oil
3 onions, chopped
5 garlic cloves, crushed
1/2 tsp ground pepper
3 large potatoes, diced
salt to taste
1 tbsp Hungarian paprika
1 yellow pepper

Brown the onions in oil until transparent, mix with the Hungarian paprika, then add some water and braise them.

Add meat, crushed garlic, salt and pepper. When the meat turns white, add some water, cover and tender.

Add water many times while the meat softens. Cook without cover and stir often in order for water to become absorbed.

Serve with diced fried potatoes and decorate with onion and paprika slices.

A Dish Of Peas

This dish can be served as a starter or eaten as main meal together with meat fillets. I simply eat them with bread, delicious.

serves 4
takes 30 minutes

800 g green peas
(fresh or frozen)
oil for sauté
salt, to taste
a pinch of marjoram
1 tbsp sugar (you may
adjust to taste)
milk enough to cover peas
3 tbsp flour as thickener
(you may adjust to taste)
parsley finely chopped

Heat some oil in a sauce pan, add green peas and cook for 5-6 min.

Next add salt, marjoram and sugar to the green peas, and stir .

Pour in the milk enough to cover peas.

Mix flour with some milk and put aside. When peas are soft, stir in the flour mixture.

Stir for a few minutes and remove from heat.

Finally add finely chopped parsley before serving.

Lecsó Hajni Style

Lecsó can be any thing you want it to be. It is very versatile. A cooked mixture of onions, yellow banana peppers, tomatoes and paprika. Add some sliced Hungarian Sausage and it can be served as an appetizer or stew. Serve it over dumplings or rice as a main course. Spoon it over scrambled eggs for breakfast. Use it as a sauce for sausage or corn meal mush. However you use it you will find it to be quite compatible with a variety of dishes. It is an ancient dish.

serves 4
takes 35 minutes

2 tbs lard or oil
2 medium onions, sliced
500 g yellow sweet paprika
seeded and sliced.
(Do not use green bell
peppers they have little
flavour and will turn to pulp)
2 large very ripe tomatoes
peeled and diced
pinch of tarragon
3 garlic cloves, mashed
1/2 tsp salt
pepper
1 tbs Hungarian Paprika
150 g smoked kolbász
(dried sausage)
finely chopped parsley

Heat lard, add sliced onion, salt, pepper, and cook over very low heat for 5 minutes.

Add yellow sweet paprika slices with a pinch of tarragon and sprinkle half of the Hungarian paprika powder (do not stir, leave the paprika on top allowing it to become absorbed) simmer for an additional 15 min.

Then add tomatoes, garlic, salt, dried sausage and the rest of the Hungarian paprika powder. Cook for 10 minutes longer.

Add salt to taste. If you are going to add dried sausage, reduce salt.

Finally add finely chopped parsley before serving. Lecsó can also be frozen.

Fried Dough, Lángos

During the long winters when Hungarians needed substantial snacks to keep their bodies fuelled, the lángos was a good choice. The smell is heavenly, they are smeared with the juice of a cut garlic clove and eaten warm. As children, we would stand impatiently around the kitchen waiting to get the first cakes out of the pan.

serves 4
takes 75 minutes

3 or 4 medium potatoes
1/2 cup warm milk, for yeast
300 g bread flour
10 g yeast
100 g lard
150 g cheese
1 1/2 cups sour cream
1/2 tsp salt
1 clove of garlic, mashed
1 tsp sugar
Hungarian Paprika

Peel the potatoes and cook in boiling salted water. Then mash them immediately. You should have about 1 1/2 cups. Cool the mashed potatoes. Mix the warm milk with the yeast and sugar. Let the starter sit for 5 or 10 minutes. Add it to mashed potatoes with flour and the salt. Start with 1 1/2 cups and add more flour to make a kneadable dough. Knead dough well. Put dough in a bowl and cover. Let dough rise in a warm place until double in bulk. For about 1 hour. Roll out the dough with a floured rolling pin on a floured board to 1 cm thick. Cut into rectangles, squares or circles. Prick with a knife to keep big bubbles from forming.

Melt lard in a frying pan so it is at least 2 cm deep. Fry lángos over medium heat. If the lard is too hot they will burn, if the lard is to cool the lángos will absorb too much lard. Watch them closely. Let them get a nice colour.

When they are done, rub each lángos with a mashed clove of garlic and sprinkle with salt, sour cream or cheese or Hungarian Paprika. Good along with bean or lentil soups, or a snack with beer or wine.

Stuffed Green Peppers

Töltött paprika are a common Hungarian dish, particularly at the end of the summer when both peppers and tomatoes are in season. The best kind of peppers to use in this recipe are the sweet, long, pale yellow ones. They are often called "Hungarian peppers" or "banana peppers". Slow, low cooking is the secret.

serves 6
takes 75 minutes

12 peppers
500 g pork mince
100 g rice, parboiled
1,5 kg tomatoes
50 g sugar
2 tsp salt
100 g lard
2 tbsp flour
2 tsp marjoram
1 egg
1/2 tsp ground pepper
1 big onion
1 clove garlic, finely chopped
2 tbsp parsley

Cut off the tops of peppers and put them aside. Remove the seeds.

Sauté half of the onion in lard. In mixing bowl, place the ground meat, browned onion, raw egg, simmered rice, salt, pepper, marjoram, garlic and parsley. Mix well using your hands.

Stuff peppers, using the entire meat mixture. If you have some left-over, make a few balls. Set peppers up-right in cooking pot and add chopped tops of peppers over the peppers.

Prepare the roux and dilute with the juice of the boiled and crushed tomatoes, salt, the rest of the onion and the sugar. Add some water if needed.

Add this to the stuffed peppers and simmer slowly and well for about an hour.

Hungarian Fruity Chicken Breasts

serves 6
takes 60 minutes

6 whole chicken breasts,
boned
300 g butter
1 cup diced apple
1/2 cup coarsely chopped
nuts
1/2 cup golden raisins
1 cup crushed pineapple
1 cup soft bread crumbs
toasted
1 tsp salt
1 tsp cinnamon
1/2 tsp nutmeg
¼ tsp ginger
¼ tsp ground cloves
2 apricot, sliced
2 cup kiwi, sliced

FOR FILLING melt 150 g butter in a pan; sauté diced apple and chopped nuts 10 minutes.

Remove from heat. Add raisins, 1/2 cup drained crushed pineapple (reserve remaining pine- apple), toasted bread crumbs, 1/2 teaspoon salt, cinnamon, nutmeg, ginger and cloves.

Cut the chicken breasts open for the filling. Season the inside with salt. Place stuffing inside of each breast; fold the sides over, and seal with toothpicks.

Place remaining 150 g butter in baking pan lined with foil; place in oven (150°C) until melted, for about 5 minutes.

Place breasts top-side down in melted butter; return pan to oven and bake chicken for 25 minutes.

Turn the chicken breasts over and place apricot, kiwi slices and remaining crushed pineapple on breasts and bake for another 20 minutes.

Serve with steamed rice and fresh fruits.

Layered Potato Casserole

„Rakott Krumpli" is a typical Hungarian main dish, hence, it will be difficult to find in the menus of the elegant Hungarian restaurants. This dish is much more common within the kitchens of Hungarian families or perhaps in ‚less-expensive' Hungarian self-service eating outlets.

serves 4
takes 45 minutes

1 kg potatoes
5 eggs, hard -boiled
150 g Hungarian dried smoked sausage, sliced
2 1/2 cup sour cream
50 g smoked bacon, diced
salt to taste

Cook unpeeled potatoes in salt water until tender then peel and slice.

Peel the hard-boiled eggs and slice them.

Fry the Hungarian sausage and bacon for 3 minutes.

Now make layers with the ingredients in a greased pan or a deep casserole. Start with a layer of potatoes, salt the layer and sprinkle with the lard of the fried sausage and bacon. Add a few pieces of sausage and bacon and slices of eggs, put some sour cream on top and cover with a layer of potatoes. Add salt and some lard. Repeat the egg and sausage/bacon layer and cover with potatoes.

Spread 1-2 tablespoon sour cream over top.

Bake in a medium heat oven for 35-40 minutes.

Serve with beetroot or any other pickles.

Squash With Stew

Who would have thought that the humble squash could be transformed into a culinary delicacy. Combined with stew (pörkölt), this squash dish reaches undreamt of heights.

serves 4
takes 85 minutes

STEW: 500 g of cubed beef
1 large onion, chopped
1 tbsp oil, 1 clove garlic
1 tomato, diced
1 yellow paprika, chopped
2 tbsp Hungarian paprika
fresh Hungarian hot paprika
(chilli), as much as you like to
make it pungent
salt to taste
SQUASH: 2 tbsp butter
1 medium squash, peeled
seeded and cut into strips
1 tbsp finely chopped onion
1 tbsp vinegar
pinch of dill seed (finely crushed
or chopped fresh dill leaves)
salt and pepper to taste
1 tsp sugar
1 tsp paprika
1 1/2 tsp flour

MAKE THE STEW: Chop the onion, the chillies and the garlic, if used. Cube the meat. Chop the tomato. Sautè the onion, chilli and garlic in some oil until the onion is transparent. Remove from heat to add the paprika and stir it in. Add the tomato and the meat and about a cupful of water or stock.

Transfer to Crock-pot and cook slowly until meat is tender and the sauce has thickened. Add salt and chilli.

MAKE THE SQUASH: Melt three-quarters of the butter in a frying pan. Add the squash strips and cook, turning frequently, until the squash is soft and melted.

Take the squash out with a slotted spoon, add the onion to the pan and fry until softened.

Stir in the vinegar, dill, salt, pepper, sugar and paprika, then return the squash to the pan. Mix well and cook gently for 2 minutes.

Mash the remaining butter with the flour to make a paste and add to the pan in small pieces, stirring well. Simmer until thickened, then serve with pörkölt (stew).

Buttered Lentils

This dish is usually served in the fall and winter months. This is another one of those hearty peasant dishes that is a complete meal by itself. Serve it with some crusty bread, a chunk of boiled eggs and a good dark beer.

serves 4
takes 25 minutes

500 g of Lentils, dried
1 medium onion, minced
2 garlic cloves, mashed
250 g butter, unsalted
salt, to taste
1/2 tsp Hungarian paprika powder
 1/2 tsp black pepper
1/2 tsp sugar
1 tsp mustard
1/2 tsp vinegar (10%)
3 tbsp flour
2 small bay leaves
3 tbsp oil
4 eggs, boiled

Wash the lentils and soak them in water overnight.

Drain. Using a large pot, add bay leaves, drained lentils, salt and enough water to cover.

Cook until done - about 20 minutes. Sauté the onion and flour in the oil for 5 minutes.

Add garlic, black pepper and Hungarian paprika and stir.

Add the onion-flour-garlic-paprika mix, mustard and sugar to the cooked lentils and boil a few minutes longer.

While the lentils are still very hot stir in the butter.

Add vinegar just before serving and adjust salt.

Shin Stew With Tarhonya

The secret of the real traditional Beef Shin Stew lies in its simplicity. Paprika, in generous amounts makes a great deal of sense, as well exercised tough muscles like shin (lower leg) develop a great deal of flavour. Cook such meat slowly at simmering temperature to make the meat tender with a rich ‚beefy' flavour. Tarhonya is mainly used in the Hungarian kitchen. It is a kind of pasta and can be bought "ready to cook", like noodles.

serves 4
takes 100 minutes

500 g shin of beef, cut into
4-5 cm cubes
freshly ground black pepper
1/4 cup lard
2 onions, diced
1 yellow pepper, chopped
1 tomato, chopped
2 garlic cloves, crushed
1 1/2 tbsp sweet, Hungarian
paprika
1/2 tsp ground cumin
hot paprika and -salt to taste

Heat the lard in a cauldron or heavy soup pot. Brown onion in the lard. Add Hungarian paprika, meat, and some water, Add water many times while the meat softens. Adjust the heat so that the stew simmers until the meat is tender, for about 1 1/2 hours. Add cumin, black pepper, yellow pepper, tomato, salt and garlic. Bring to boil and cook it for another 5 minutes. Adjust the seasoning with salt and hot Hungarian paprika. Serve with tarhonya or fried potatoes.

Stuffed Cabbage Szabolcs Style

Stuffed Cabbage is the National dish of Hungary. It consists of tightly rolled bundles of meat and rice held together by soft cabbage wrap. The rolls are piled on a bed of silky sauerkraut. Cabbage and sauerkraut combined make a mellow dish.

serves 4
takes 120 minutes

1 cabbage
1 jar or packet of sauerkraut
(do not use canned
sauerkraut)
500 g pork mince
200 g sausage
200 g smoked szalonna
(fatty bacon)
1 tsp salt
1 tbsp Hungarian paprika
1/2 tsp pepper corns
100 g rice
2 garlic cloves, mashed
2 tbsp oil or lard
2 cups sour cream
a pinch of sweet marjoram
or oregano

Rinse 1 large head of cabbage and the sauerkraut in cold water. Place the mince, the uncooked rice, paprika, garlic, salt and some oil in a mixing bowl. Mix well using your hands.

Remove the core of the cabbage. Leave head whole. Place in large pot of boiling water to wilt the outer leaves. You will be able to gently pull off whole cabbage leaves. Trim off thick centre vein of cabbage leaves. Make a pile of leaves on your workstation. Shake excess water off. Place 2 tablespoons of meat and rice mixture on a leaf (starting at the thick end) and roll it up and tuck in ends with your finger. Make as many as you can. Arrange the rolls in cooking pot. Put a few chunks of sausage and szalonna here and there between the rolls. Cover the rolls two-thirds full of water, arrange rinsed sauerkraut on top, sprinkle over the pepper corns and the sweet marjoram on top, cover and cook slowly for about 1 1/2 hours, or until the rice is tender.

Serve with fresh sour cream on top, good crusty bread and cold beer.

Hortobágy Meat Pancakes

The best-known type of meat-filled palacsinta is the Hortobágyi Palacsinta, which is filled with diced Chicken Paprikash.

makes 8
takes 100 minutes

PLAIN SAVOURY PANCAKES
200 g flour
2 eggs
400 millilitres milk
1 tbsp oil
pinch of salt
FILLING
1 large onion, finely chopped
500 g ground meat
1-2 tbsp lard
salt and pepper to taste
3 tsp Hungarian Paprika
30 g flour
100 millilitres sour cream
1/2 tomato, chopped
1/2 yellow pepper, chopped
parsley

Sauté the onions in lard until they are wilted, add meat, and stir until meat is white. Add some water, yellow pepper and tomato. Add the spices and cook covered for 40 minutes.

Separate the meat from sauce and add flour and sour cream to the sauce. Boil it for 5 minutes stirring constantly. Mince the meat.

MAKE PLAIN SAVOURY PANCAKES: Beat the eggs, milk and salt in a bowl. Add the flour slowly, stirring constantly. The mixture should not be lumpy. If a lighter mixture is preferred, substitute half of the milk with soda water. In this case, add the soda water slowly to the thick mixture, stirring constantly. Let the mixture stand for at least 30 minutes before frying the pancakes in oil.

Fill the pancakes with minced meat and roll them up.

Pour the sour cream sauce over the pancakes. Serve decorated with parsley.

Gypsy Roast

Cigánypecsenye is a traditional Hungarian pork dish. While every Hungarian cook seems to have their own method for preparing it, the dish is most commonly made with tarja (chop) or karaj (loin), and served with potatoes and crowned with a roasted slice of slab bacon.

serves 4
takes 40 minutes

1 kg pork chops or loins
300 g smoked bacon
(fatty one)
8 cloves garlic, mashed
4 big onions
1 cup flour
2 cups oil
salt to taste
1 tbsp ground pepper
3 tbsp Hungarian paprika

Cut the bacon into four equal pieces, cut in the skin and then fry. They will turn to a cockscomb shape when fried.

Take out the bacon pieces and add sliced onion, and brown in the lard (in the same pan). Pour the content of the frying pan (onion-lard mix) onto the bottom of a large baking pan as a bed for the meat.

Mix mashed garlic with oil. Pound the meat slices. Brush both sides with the garlic-oil blend. Salt and pepper and coat the slices with flour. Fry spare rib slices in hot oil for 2-3 minutes.

Place fried meat on the onion bed. Top with fried bacon pieces and bake for 20 minutes in oven.

When done, sprinkle the meat and bacon slices with Hungarian paprika. Serve with fried potatoes and vegetable slices.

Pork Fry Bakony Style

serves 6
takes 60 minutes

STEW
1,5 kg spare ribs of pork
250 g mushroom
1 yellow paprika
1 small tomato
oil, to fry meet
5 tbsp flour
1 cup of sour cream
1 onion
salt and pepper, to taste
1 tbsp Hungarian paprika
DUMPLINGS (NOKEDLI)
2 eggs
1/2 tsp salt 3/4 cup of water
2 cups all-purpose flour
1 large pot filled with salted
boiling water

Slice, pound, season with salt and pepper spare ribs of pork and coat them in flour.

Slice mushrooms, chop onion, paprika and tomato.

Fry pieces of spare rib in oil. In a separate pan, brown onion in oil, add Hungarian paprika, mushrooms, paprika and tomato. Season with salt and pepper. Simmer for 10 min.

Mix the sour cream with flour stirring constantly. The mixture should not be lumpy. Add Sour Cream mix to mushroom sauce and cook for 5 min. Spread over fried slices of meat.

Serve with dumplings.

TO MAKE DUMPLINGS place pot filled with salted water and bring to boil. Combine eggs, salt, flour and water, beating well with whisk. Add only enough flour to make a soft, sticky dough. Using a spatula press 1/2 of the batter through spaetzle maker into boiling water.

The noodles are done when they float to the top. Remove from water with large slotted spoon, and sprinkle with a tablespoon of oil.

Hungarian Meat Loaf

This Hungarian Meat Loaf, also called Stefánia szelet (Stefania slices), is so special because when cut into slices the hard boiled eggs in the middle of the loaf make decorative white and yellow rings.

serves 4
takes 80 min

3 large eggs, hard boiled
300 g mince (veal, pork)
1 large onion, chopped
2 cloves garlic, crushed
3-4 slices bacon, diced
1 large tomato, diced
6 slices white bread
1/2 tsp salt
1/2 tsp pepper
50 g lard
1/2 cup milk
flour

Fry large onion with bacon in the lard, add garlic near the end.

Mix all the meat together with onions, garlic and bacon. Place bread in a dish and pour milk over it and let soak for about 10 minutes and add to meat. Add all the other ingredients (except tomatoes) and mix.

Coat your board with flour. Lay out the mince on the board. Add the boiled eggs in the centre of mince placing them 1-2 cm distance from each other. Fold the side of the meat mix covering the eggs entirely.

Place diced tomato on the bottom of a large baking tray or heat proof dish as a bed for the meat loaf.

Bake at 180 °C for 60 minutes or until done. Check after 50 minutes of baking time and pour with lard if necessary.

Serve with buttered lentils or with fried potatoes and fresh vegetables.

Hungarian Cream Puffs

This recipe for Hungarian Cream Puffs is similar to French profiteroles. The French had a profound effect on the pastries of Hungary and Austria in the late 1800s and the connection remains strong.

makes about 12 large puffs
takes 40 minutes

1 cup water
100 g unsalted butter
cut into small pieces
1/8 tsp salt
200 g all-purpose flour
5 eggs
FILLING
150 g custard powder
1 tbsp all-purpose flour
3 eggs separated
100 g sugar
2 cups milk

Heat oven to 160 °C. Line a baking tray with parchment paper. In a medium saucepan, bring water, butter and salt to a boil. Once butter has completely melted, remove from heat and, using a wooden spoon, add flour all at once. Return to stove and stir over low heat for 2 or 3 minutes or until dough cleans sides of pan and forms a ball. Remove from heat and stir in eggs one at a time, beating well after each addition. Batter should be smooth and glossy and cling to the spoon. For mini puffs, using a cookie scoop, portion out mounds of dough on baking sheet.

Bake minis for 20 minutes until puffy and golden brown on top and bottom. Let puffs cool completely before filling. Cut the bottom off puff, remove the moist interior, fill with cream, level, replace the bottom. **TO MAKE THE FILLING** mix custard powder, flour, egg yolks and sugar. Stir well until foamy. Add milk and cook, stirring constantly until thickened. Beat egg whites until stiff and add to custard. Serve immediately or refrigerate until ready to be eaten. Hungarian Cream Puffs don't hold well - the puff becomes soggy - so eat them the day they are made.

Snow Kipferl

Snow kipferls are small biscuits shaped like a crescent moon. They are particularly popular in Hungary, where they are part of the culinary delights of the Christmas season. It is a unique experience wandering through the Christmas markets in the snow. It is literally a feast for all senses - the glow of lights and candles, the smell of roasted chestnuts, and the taste of warm Christmas biscuits. Baking Christmas biscuits is a family activity to be enjoyed on wintry days, when it is snowing outside.

makes 60 Kipferls
takes 60 minutes

500 g plain flour
1/2 cup milk
20 g yeast
200 g cold unsalted butter
100 g icing sugar
1 egg, a pinch of salt
1 packet vanilla sugar
FILLING
100 g ground walnuts
15 g honey
15 g raisins
zest of 1 lemon
¼ cup water
FOR COATING THE KIPFERL AFTER BAKING
60 g icing sugar
2 packets of vanilla sugar

Sieve the flour into a bowl. Cut the cold butter into slices and mix with the flour. Add icing sugar, salt, vanilla sugar, milk, yeast, and egg to the mixture.

Knead the dough on a pastry board. Let the dough rest for 25 min.

Grease a baking tray. Preheat the oven to 180 °C. Roll out the dough to about 0.5 cm thick. Cut out triangle shapes finishing the whole dough.

FILLING: Mix walnuts, raisins, lemon crest. Boil sugar with honey and add walnut mix. Divide the filling for the triangle shapes. Fill each triangle and shape them to crescents which are placed on the baking tray, and bake them for 10-15 minutes until they are a light golden brown.

Immediately after baking, roll the crescents in a mixture of icing sugar and vanilla sugar.

Noodle Pie

The original recipe was published by a journalist under the alias Lucullus, at the beginning of the 1900's in „The Cookbook of Greater Hungary," with the following quotation on the cover: „Collected from the recipes of the best Hungarian housewives, by Lucullus." This is traditional Hungarian „noodle pie" dessert.

makes 18
takes 60 minutes

FILLING
*150 g dry vermicelli
(soup pasta)
500 g curd cheese
100 g sugar
1 cup sour cream
15 g butter
6 eggs, separated
1 lemon zest
2 tsp vanilla extract
20 g raisins*

DOUGH
*1 Package of strudel pastry
(Phyllo pastry)
4 tbsp butter, melted*

Put the vermicelli in boiling water and cook for 5 minutes.

Make a tasty cottage cheese pancake filling (curd cheese, sour cream, egg yolk, sugar, butter, egg whites beaten, vanilla extract, raisins, and lemon zest).

Place a layer of the strudel pastry in a buttered baking pan. Then spread butter over strudel, spread thin layer of cottage cheese filling over top, cover with a layer of vermicelli, then strudel pastry again, butter, filling, vermicelli, strudel pastry, repeat this order three times in all.

Brush the top strudel pastry layer with egg yolk and bake until nice and golden brown at the top, cut and serve hot.

Gundel's Pancakes

This delicious and decadent dessert is made from a very old pancake recipe originating from a famous century-old Budapest restaurant, called Gundel's. The original owner, Karoly Gundel, created this pancake. It is flambéed at the table and served with warm chocolate sauce. It's divine!

serves 4-6
takes 60 minutes

CHOCOLATE SAUCE

50 ml rum, 50 g cocoa
3 tbsp sugar
2 tbsp flour, 3 egg yolks
200 ml milk
100 ml double cream
100 g dark chocolate, chopped
20 g vanilla sugar

PANCAKES

2 eggs, beaten
400 ml milk
240 g semolina flour
50 g butter
60 g butter for frying
pinch of salt, 10 g sugar

FILLING

180 g walnuts, 60 g raisins
100 g sugar
20 g (2 tbsp) candied orange peel, 100 ml rum or brandy
pinch of cinnamon powder
100 ml double cream

FOR THE CHOCOLATE SAUCE beat the cocoa, sugar, flour and yolks together. Bring the milk and cream to a boil and pour over the yolk mixture, whisk until smooth. Return to the heat and cook gently, stirring, until the custard thickens. Remove from heat and add the chocolate and rum, stirring until combined. Keep sauce warm while you cook the pancakes.
FOR THE PANCAKES whisk the eggs, sugar, pinch of salt and milk into the semolina flour until you have a smooth batter. Let stand for 10 minutes. The consistency should be like pouring cream - you may need to add a touch more milk. Fry the pancakes in butter and set aside.
FOR THE FILLING. Soak the raisins and finely candied orange peels in rum for 24 hours. Grate the walnuts, but not too finely. Bring the cream to a boil, add the sugar, nuts, a pinch of cinnamon and drained raisins, the orange peel and cook it into a paste. (If necessary add a little milk.) Let the mixture cool partially and add the rum. Fill in each pancake and fold into four in triangular shapes. Heat a large frying pan with the butter and add the filled pancakes, frying gently to warm them through. Cook on both sides. Place them on a preheated flameproof platter. Pour the chocolate sauce over the crepes at the last minute before serving. Traditionally in the restaurant they are sprinkled with rum and flamed at the table before being finished with the chocolate sauce.

Hungarian Chestnut Puree

It would not be exaggeration to say that sweetened Chestnut puree flavoured with abundant rum is a staple food in Hungary.

makes about 4 cups
takes 5 minutes
(store-bought method)

1 kg chestnuts or 600 g
store-bought chestnut puree
200 g vanilla sugar
1/2 litre double cream
1- 4 tbsp rum
1/2 litre water

Boil the chestnuts in water till tender, drain and pour cold water over top. This makes the chestnuts easy to peel. Take the outer and inner skin off and put the chestnuts through a mincer or Moulinette, using the finest blade.

Make a thick syrup of the vanilla sugar with 1/2 litre water, and flavour with the rum, then mix with the chestnut puree.

When cooled, coat with a slightly sweetened whipped cream.

Chill before serving.

If using store-bought chestnut purée, press through a sieve and add a few tablespoons of rum to loosen it up a bit before introducing the whipped cream.

Cherry Strudel

When my Grandma made strudel, she would have all hands available helping. The dining room table would be covered with a white cloth on which the strudel dough would be pulled thin until you could read a newspaper through it. Today we can purchase strudel pastry which saves a lot of back breaking work. Here is a simple way of making good Hungarian strudel. It is as good as homemade but requires much less work.

makes 18 slices
takes 50 minutes

1 Package of strudel pastry
(Phyllo pastry)
3 tbsp of butter, melted
500 g cherries, cored
50 g finely ground walnuts
30 g raisins
1 tsp cinnamon
5 tbsp sugar
4 tbsp bread crumbs
1 large clean kitchen towel
(used to roll strudel)
1 egg

Lay out clean wet towel and put sheets of strudel pastry on top. Butter the strudel pastry. Sprinkle bread crumbs, sugar, cinnamon, raisins and walnuts.

Place cherries on top and take the edge of the towel nearest you and slowly start to make a big roll by pulling up and towards you.

Then tuck the ends of the strudel underneath itself.

Beat an egg and brush the pastry with it and bake at 180 °C degrees for about 30 minutes.

Cool and cut into slices and dust with powdered sugar. You can vary the filling by adding raisins. If you add raisins you must first soften them in hot water and then dry them before using.

When you lay out the strudel pastry sheets you will want to have at least 2 or 3 layers buttered on top of one another.

Semolina Milk Pudding

Tejbegriz is a sweet, tasty and simple Hungarian remedy for the hungry one.

serves 3-4
takes 15 min

200 g semolina
1 liter milk
1/2 tsp cinnamon powder
4 tbsp sugar
fresh strawberries,
blueberries on top
(optional)

Pour the milk into a pan and bring to a boil, add the semolina and stir steadily until it reaches a pudding-like consistency.

Add sugar, according to one's taste.

Serve with plenty of cinnamon powder sprinkled over the pudding and with fresh fruits such as strawberries or blueberries overtop.

Curd Cheese Cake Rákóczi Style

This dessert is also known as Rákóczi Style curd cheesecake after János Rákóczi (1897-1966), a Hungarian chef who was believed to have created the dessert. Some have lattice-type tops made of meringue.

makes 16 slices
takes 50 minutes

CRUST
300 g all-purpose flour
100 g icing sugar
200 g butter
2 egg yolks
1/2 lemon zest

FILLING
750 g dry curd farmers cheese
5 tbsp sugar
3 egg yolks
1 tsp vanilla
1/2 lemon zest
100 g raisins.

MERINGUE TOPPING
5 egg whites
5 tbsp icing sugar
5 tbsp apricot filling or jam

Preheat oven to 180 °C. Mix flour with butter, add powder sugar, egg yolks and lemon zest.

Roll out dough to about 1 cm thick. Half bake the dough for about 15 min.

Mix curd cheese, sugar, egg yolks, vanilla, raisins and lemon zest. Get half baked dough out of the oven and smear curd cheese mix (curd cheese, sugar, egg yolks, vanilla, lemon zest and raisins) over top and place back into the oven.

When almost ready, remove and reduce temperature to 120 °C - 140 °C. Beat egg white with sugar and smear on top. Either pipe meringue over cheesecake surface in lattice-type rows or spread it evenly over the entire surface, using a spatula to make swirls.

Bake 15 minutes or until meringue is light brown.

Decorate with apricot filling or jam. Cool completely before cutting into squares.

Honey Cake (Mézes-Krémes)

This unusual method for cooking this „torte" is labour and time intensive but really worth the effort.

makes 20 slices
takes 60 minutes

TORTE
60 g unsalted butter
150 g sugar
4 tbsp sour cream
2 tbsp dark wildflower honey
500 g all-purpose flour
1 tsp baking soda
2 eggs
FILLING
5 tbsp semolina
3 cups milk
200 g unsalted butter
250 g icing sugar
1 cup apricot or
sour cherry jam

TO MAKE THE TORTE put all the torte ingredients in a small bowl. Mix thoroughly by hand. Make a dough, kneading a few minutes until the dough is smooth. Divide into 4 balls. Cover and let rest for 30 minutes. Using a rolling pin, flatten each ball and roll out into a 25 by 37 cm rectangle. Place on 4 greased baking trays and bake in a preheated oven at 165 °C until the surface is golden brown, for about 18 to 20 minutes. Remove the sheets from the oven and let stand overnight at room temperature.

TO MAKE THE FILLING cook the semolina in milk for 5 minutes stirring constantly until thickened. Let cool slightly. Mix the butter with sugar then add it to the cooked semolina.

Place half of the filling on the first pre-baked sheet of dough. Put the second sheet of dough on top of the first and spread on the apricot or sour cherry jam. Then put the third sheet on top, spread on the remaining filling, and finally top with the last sheet.

Cover and refrigerate overnight. Cut into small squares.

Gerbeaud

This is an original Hungarian dessert, created by a French confectioner who lived and worked in Hungary. This dessert is simply excellent.

serves 10
takes 150 minutes

DOUGH
200 g flour
100 g margarine
20 g sugar
1 egg yolk
8 g yeast
1 g baking powder
pinch of salt
5 tbsp milk

FILLING
600 g apricot jam
200 g ground walnut
160 g sugar
1 tsp cinnamon
zest of one lemon
10 g vanilla sugar

TOP
100 g dark chocolate,
broken into pieces

Mix all the dough ingredients together and knead well. You should get a firm, not soft, shapeable dough. Cut the dough into 5 similar-sized pieces. Put in baking paper to a medium baking tin. On floured surface, roll out one of the dough pieces to the size of the baking tin then place inside. Mix together the ground walnut, vanilla sugar, cinnamon powder, grated lemon zest and sugar. Put one quarter of the jam on the first layer of dough. Sprinkle the layer of jam with the one quarter of the walnut-sugar etc. mix. Roll out the second piece of dough. Put it on as the next layer and the jam-walnut-sugar mix. Repeat it 3 more times. When finished prick through the layers with a fork. Cover the baking tin with a tea towel and allow the dough to rise the for 1 and half hours, in room temperature. Heat the oven to 180 °C and bake the cake for 45-50 min, until the top is light-brown. Take the cake out from the oven, allow to cool for an hour.

FOR THE CHOCOLATE TOPPING: Melt the chocolate. Turn the cake upside down and put the chocolate on the top of it and smooth it with a wide knife. Allow to cool and firm completely then cut into narrow slices.

Hungarian Jam Pudding

Another piece of Hungarian excellence. A really filling, rich dessert. Everybody knows this delicacy, but those who don't, try it as soon as possible!

serves 12
takes 90 minutes

250 g milk loaf
200 g apricot jam
MILK MIXTURE
500 ml milk
zest of 1 lemon
zest of 1 orange
1 tbsp vanilla extract
EGG YOLK MIXTURE
5 egg yolks
70 g sugar
STEWED APPLE
600 g apple
30 g sugar
juice of 1 lemon and 1 orange
pinch of ground cinnamon
EGG WHITE MIXTURE
70 g sugar
5 egg whites

First butter a 23 x 33 cm baking tray. Slice the milk loaf, then put the slices in a bowl. For the milk mixture, pour milk into a bowl, add the orange and the lemon's grated rind, the vanilla extract and boil the mixture. When the mixture is boiled, pour it over the milk loaf slices. Beat the egg yolks with sugar, and pour over the milk loaf slices. Mix the milk loaf slices well with the milk and the egg mixture, and place them evenly in the baking tray. Peel the apples, slice them, and stew them under a lid, on low heat, with the lemon juice, orange juice, sugar and cinnamon. Place the stewed apples in the baking tray, on top of the milk loaf slices.

Bake in the oven for about 20 minutes, at 180°C. Then spread it with half of the apricot jam.

Prepare the egg white mixture. Whisk the egg whites with the sugar and a pinch of salt until very stiff. With a wooden spoon, very gently, stir the rest of the apricot jam in the egg whites, in a way that the mixture remains „striped". Spread the egg white mixture on the top of the apples, „thorn" it, sprinkle with castor sugar, and bake it at 170°C for about 10 minutes.

Floating Island

Floating Island is made of egg white dumplings served floating on a milky custard sauce. Some variations use a thicker sauce, served on top of the dumplings, but usually the milk mix is thin, almost liquid, and the dumplings „float" on top.

serves 6
takes 25 minutes

1 litre milk, to boil
6 eggs, separated
6 tbsp sugar
1 tsp vanilla

Beat egg whites until stiff.

Boil milk and add half of sugar.

Drop tablespoonsful of egg whites into boiling milk.

Turn on other side after a few seconds.

Take out boiled whites and place in a flat dish. Continue this until all whites are used.

Put egg yolks and rest of sugar in a bowl and beat well. Add yolk mixture to boiling milk and cook for one minute.

Add vanilla. Cool.

Put the egg fluffs on top of the custard.

Serve cold.

Wasp Nests

makes 18 nests
takes 100 minutes

DOUGH
30 g yeast
500 g flour
250 ml lukewarm milk
pinch of sugar
pinch of salt
7 egg yolks
FILLING
200 g butter
230 g sugar
200 g grounded walnut
FOR THE BASTING
200 g double cream

Start with combining the yeast, sugar, milk and the 2 tbsp flour, cover and set aside until it starts to bubble.

Measure the flour into a large bowl, make a well in the middle and add the egg yolks, salt and the yeast mixture. Combine ingredients. Knead until smooth and elastic. Place in a floured bowl, cover and let rise in a warm place until doubled, about 30 minutes.

Once the dough has risen, turn it out onto a lightly floured surface and roll it into a rectangle (about 1 cm thick).

FOR FILLING mix butter with sugar and grounded walnut until foamy. Spread dough with filling and roll up from the long side. Cut into 3 cm slices and place with cut side down in a greased baking pan. Cover and let rise again, until doubled, about 30 minutes. Bake at 200 degrees C until golden brown (about 25 minutes). When the rolls start to gain a slight color, take out from oven and baste with double cream.

Put back in the oven for another 5 minutes.

Plum Dumplings

Hungarian plum dumplings - szilvás gombóc - can be eaten as dessert, main dish or side dish. Some men have contests to see how many they can consume during a single sitting. Thirty is not unheard of, though four is a usual serving. You can not eat just one. Some Hungarian mothers make them large with a lot of dough, others use less dough.

serves 18 dumplings
takes 40 minutes

5 medium potatoes, peeled, boiled, mashed and cooled
1 tsp salt
2 1/2 cups all-purpose flour
18 plums, washed and pitted
4 tbsp oil
1 1/2 cups very fine bread crumbs
1/4 cup caster sugar

After peeling the potatoes, cook them in salted water.

Filter the potatoes and mash with a potato masher. Add flour and knead together quickly.

Form dough into a thick roll and cut into 18 slices.

Put plums in the middle of the squares and roll them up by putting the 4 corners together.

Place the dumplings into boiling water and cook until they rise to the top of the water.

In the meantime, brown the bread crumbs in heated oil, add some sugar.

Roll the cooked dumplings in the bread crumbs and serve sprinkled with caster sugar.

Poppy Seed Strudel

These cakes predate Christianity as the poppy was dedicated to the Moon goddess. (Opium-sleep). The recipes were handed down by the women. These cakes are now usually made around Christmas time when fancy baking is typically done. These cakes can be wrapped in foil and stored in the freezer after they are baked.

makes 4
takes 180 minutes

POPPY SEED FILLING
450 g of freshly ground poppy seeds (finely)
240 g sugar
1 cup boiled milk
1/4 cup melted butter
2 tbsp peach jam
100 g raisins
2 tbsp lemon zest

DOUGH
800 g flour
240 g sugar
1 cup lukewarm water
2 eggs, slightly beaten
2 cake yeasts, regular or dry
1/2 cup soft butter
1 tsp salt

POPPY SEED FILLING: Cook filling in bowl using only 3/4 cup of boiled milk, It should be thick. If not spreadable use the rest of milk. Divide into 4 portions, one for each dough rollup.

MAKE DOUGH: Crumble yeast in bowl, add water and sugar stirring till mixture liquefies. Blend flour and butter with wire pastry blender. Mix well, mix in eggs, salt and yeast. Mix until dough is smooth and leaves the side of the bowl clean. DO NOT LET RISE. Divide into four portions and roll each out in a rectangular shape, spread with filling and roll up like a Jelly Roll. Brush the rolls with egg yolks then put them aside for 20 minutes in a cool place. Prick rolls with toothpick on top and the sides to keep from splitting while baking. Place in greased baking pans.

Bake at once in 180 °C oven about 30 to 45 min. or until brown.

These cakes can be wrapped in foil and stored in the freezer after they are baked.

Published by CasteloArt Kft.
www.casteloart.hu

Text copyright © Ildikó Kolozsvári
Photographs copyright © István Hajni
Food decoration © Ildikó Kolozsvári

Designed and edited by
Bear Books Publishing,
István Hajni

BEAR
BOOKS

István Hajni would like to thank the following
who have helped directly in making this book:
Ottó István Hajni (my Dad),
Alexandra Tutunzis (my Mum),
Chris Tutunzis, Randy Simor,
Goran Milosevic

ISBN 978-963-88963-6-0

Printed in Italy

FRONT COVER: Cherry Strudel

Ildikó Kolozsvári